Real Estate Investing:

Master Rentals — and Build Your Empire And Passive Income With Apartment Rentals, Multifamily Homes And Commercial Real Estate Flipping

By

Income Mastery

Table of Contents

Introduction

Every single person that wants a fix for their financial needs long term looking for that magic solution. Many people do not have a clue on what they should be doing, or where they should start. Utilizing real estate is one of the top proven methods of a guaranteed success on a long term basis. Look at it like having your own little real estate empire. Real estate is not an exception when it comes to fluctuations on the market. It will continue to climb as far as the value. This means that there will always be a way to increase your overall investment. We are going to dive into how you are going to build your own little empire and secure a good future for you and your family. Your investment success is waiting.

Understanding Apartment Rentals 101

When renting an apartment, there is a fee that is paid in order to use the property. It is a fee paid to the owner in order to dwell inside of the home, it is called rent. You are able to live in the space that is outlined in the terms of a lease agreement. There will be aspects that are covered under the terms of the fee. There will also be late fees accumulated due to rent being paid after the date specified in the lease. There may even be restrictions. Rent works differently from landlord to landlord. It is crucial to ensure you understand all of the terms before you sign a lease agreement.

Understanding the Payment Terms of an Apartment

Should you rent an apartment, you will pay a specified amount for the rent to the landlord. It will be completely outlined and detailed in the lease agreement. Rent is paid on one specific day on the month; every month. The rent amount will remain the same throughout the term of the lease. The length of the lease agreement is typically for one year. However, there are other apartment owners that will agree to a shorter or longer lease agreement term. Should you be late with your rent, the landlord may or may not allow a grace period. The grace period is a specified increment of time after the payment date that will ensure you do not get a late fee. If you pay your rent after the grace period ends, you will ensure a late fee. The amount of the fee will be listed in your lease.

What is it that Rent Buys You?

When you rent an apartment you are renting the space, but this rental prices will not pay for some of the other aspects of the agreement. There are other bills that you may be required to pay. For example, there are many places that will not pay for your utilities and some types of maintenance. You will possibly be liable for paying your own cable, internet, gas, and water bills. There are many apartment complexes that offer different aspects on the rental agreement. They will be listed. These items are called amenities. Amenities includes things like a pool, gym, or even a covered parking garage.

Understanding Other Fees

Once you have decided on an apartment, it is extremely important to understand the other fees that can be included in the lease agreements. You may be subject to paying a deposit, as well as one month of rent in advance. This will ensure that you are on good terms with the apartment complex. Some landlords may ask that you pay the last month's rent in advance. There may be other types of fees or fines included with the specific rental property. Make sure that you look over and understand them all.

When someone is on the hunt for an apartment, they will look at everything from the water pressure strength to the size of the closets. However, the primary focus will be on the amount of rent that is paid monthly. They will make sure that they get the best value and will ensure that it fits in their financial budget.

Application Fee

When a person does an application for an apartment, they will need to fill out an application. Typically, this application will have a fee attached to it. It will be so that a background check can be conducted to ensure "good" people are renting the apartments. No landlord wants felons living in their apartment complex. It is just asking for trouble. Landlords also run credit checks, which also cost money. This is to ensure that the tenant will pay the rent that is agreed upon.

Application fee can really mean anything, depending on the potential landlord. It will typically cover the cost of running a history on finances, credit check, and to see if there have been any evictions on their background.

The application fee that is paid is non-refundable. The application fee is not refunded even if the tenant is denied. This is because the money is used to run the checks. However, there are limitations in most states that limit the amount a landlord is able to charge the tenant for the application fee. It will vary from state to state.

Background Check

Before a tenant is given permission to move into the apartment, the future landlord will run a background check to ensure that the tenant is not a criminal. At times, this will be included in the application fee. However, often times it is not due to the employment and credit check being included. This is normally done for other adults living in the apartment that is not on the lease.

Security Deposit

This is the money that the tenant will give to the landlord to make sure that the tenant does not leave any major damage or steal anything from the apartment when they move out. If the apartment is in the same condition as when the tenant moved in, then the security deposit will be given back to the tenant upon viewing the unit. The security deposit normally equals two to three times the amount of rent.

If there is no destruction caused in the apartment, the tenant will get all of the deposit back.

In the bigger cities, the security deposit has been phased out due to deposit free type of tenting. It is an agreement for the tenant and the landlord to both carry insurance. This means both of them are responsible for any damage that has been done.

First and Last Months Rental Payment

In addition, the landlord may require an added type of deposit that is equal to the payment of two rental fees. This will cover the landlord should the tenant decide to skip out without paying the rent that was agreed upon. If the tenant moves out before the rental agreement time is up and the rent is not paid, this will cover those fees. If the tenant stays and pays, then the landlord will give it back.

Move In Apartment Fees

There has been a new fee popping up in the apartment real estate market. This is move in costs. This fee covers changing of the locks from the previous tenant, putting the new name in the mailbox or the buzzer, and other things that need to be changed over from the last tenant. This is a non-refundable fee and is not used to fix anything that is broken.

Parking Fees

Whether or not the tenant has parking access in a lot, garage, driveway, or a specified assigned street parking, there is a parking fee that is typically a one time charge. This only covers the parking spot reservation and nothing more. However, it can also be used to repave, repaint, or even rearrange different parking spaces. There may be new codes or a permit sticker that is needed.

Pet Deposit and Fees

If the tenant is planning on bringing a pet into the unit, or even getting a new pet, it is expected that there will be an additional fee or deposit. There will be a specific amount due upon the pet moving into the unit. This is a non-refundable fee normally; however, when the tenant moves out if there is no damage, then the fee can be given back to the tenant.

Why Would I Want to Be an Apartment Landlord?

A huge benefit of owning an apartment complex is the quantity of the units included. It is a wonderful way to make sure that you have a big enough income generated on a monthly basis. Apartments are a great investment for those that are looking to work with a management company. You can put your unites together to form a good business partnership.

Advantages of Being a Landlord

There are many advantages to being a landlord. These advantages are so big that it tends to turn a typical person into an entrepreneur dreamer. It all falls down to having money coming in on a regular basis.

- Income from the renters is the biggest advantage there is. The rental properties will offer you a direct stream of income. The monthly rental checks will go straight into the bank account sat up for your real estate business. Ideally you will get more than just the offset of the cost of the rental properties. A good example of this is if you own a home that you will rent out for one thousand dollars a month, this home will then bring in twelve thousand a year. This money will go into your bank account. It is very difficult to argue with an income stream of this nature.

- You will receive income based on the property's value growth. Since you own the home or units, you will stand to take in an increase for the value of the property over time due to the changing demands in the location. This happens even if the property itself does not change. This is going to be a variable type of income. It will depend on the area where the property exists. There are some areas may stay flat.

- Sweat equity is another value that adds to the property. It is when your properties are upgraded, and you are able to charge more for the property or properties. It could be an amenity that is added to the apartment complex like a pool or covered garage.

What is a Multi-Family Home and How Does it Work?

The multi-family home is just one single home; however, there are multiple units in this one location. The wonderful part about a multi-family home is that you are able to have a steady income stream depending on how many units are rented out. When you decide to work with one of these types of homes, it will offer you a way to make sure that the mortgage on this property is completely paid, all the while adding money to your own account. If you choose to occupy the dwelling as well, then your home payment will be paid, along with receiving income.

What is Commercial Real Estate Anyway?

This type of property is defined as a property that produces income for the owner. Commercial real estate can be any type of property and is able to include any of these:

1. A gas station located in a neighborhood.
2. An apartment building or complex.
3. A skyscraper, office plaza, or office building.
4. A laundromat or car wash.

The specific reason this investment is called commercial is the fact that it will incur income for the investor. It will make sure you have a continuous income stream to financially set you free. There are five different categories that you can find just about every investor using when it comes to commercial properties. They are:

1. Office buildings.
2. Retail buildings.
3. Multi-family homes.
4. Different types of land.
5. Miscellaneous properties.

There is a tremendous amount of money to be made using commercial real estate. In different positions there are people making anywhere from $80,000 up to $250,000 yearly. That is definitely nothing to scoff at. However, when you are wanting to make that type of money, there are three roles that you should fall into.

1. **Investor**: Every successful investor builds their wealth through a long term type of ownership and consistently build their portfolios. A person can save enough money for one down payment on a cheaper apartment complex building. The income that is generated through this property will help the investor accumulate more income to spend on purchasing more properties. Adding more value to the property will also offer more income from the units. This means that the investor will utilize the flow of cash to invest in more properties.
2. **Developer**: Becoming a developer is a good way to make a lot of money in the real estate industry. Due to the money making

potential there are many people who begin their careers working as a developer. They anticipate learning enough in order to open their own real estate firm. Many fail to realize that developing is of the highest risk when it comes to real estate. They bear the risk of losing equity, and going into debt.

3. **Broker**: A broker that is good will have the potential to earn a much higher amount of money per year. Typically, they will make about $250,000 within the first two years of entering the game of commercial real estate. The brokers that are the most successful in commercial real estate will earn about seven figures every single year. When you are a broker, your money comes from commission. It is similar to being an investor or a developer, but you do not make the money in the very beginning. Typically, it will be the second year where the money will come in. The difference between being a broker and the other two is that there is a high income that is achieved without any risk of your own capital. With this position, you will earn money using your time and effort. There is a common misconception when it comes to being a broker. It is that being a broker means you just deal with sales. Yes, it does deal with

sales; however, so do many of the other professions. A good broker will be an integral part of the client's business. They will advise and offer different opinions on the types of investments, ways to control certain expenses, as well as offer suggestions on renovations and financing structures. They will be an amazing source of leads for attorneys, lenders, inspectors, appraisers, and the other types of vendors.

What Are Common Misconceptions About Commercial Real Estate?

Many ideas that people have about commercial real estate is wrong when it involves buying and selling. This industry is definitely evolving, but there are many people that are not keeping up with the new trends. What the norm was a decade ago has changed over time. Two major key factors are properties are more efficient and there is the use of technology. You need to be aware of some aspects when you decide to be in investing:

1. Real estate is not a scheme to get rich. It is crucial to know that there will be money made over time, but only by making good decisions. You will not become a millionaire overnight without some hard work.

2. One thing to consider is that some investors are not just in it for money. There are landlords that actually care about their tenants. They will work with their tenants to ensure they help them with flexibility on the rental policies.

3. Many people think that tenants do not have any rights. This is completely false. Many states offer a very clear outline of their laws to protect tenants. One rule is if the landlord chooses to evict a tenant, then the tenant does not have to get out right away. They will be given at least 30 days to figure out their situation.

4. There is a myth that brick -and-mortar retail options are being replaced by the e-commerce boom. In reality, retail remains extremely vital to our economic stability. E-commerce has just added in some more convenient options for shopping. Sales that are done in person still hold 91 percent of all retail sales. Consumers typically look for a shopping experience that will be different from the typical transactional type of format. Stores that are able to offer a sensory type of experiences have the ability to sell more due to the ability to offer a different experience than the internet.

5. Foreign investors have not soured on the United States commercial real estate like the myth suggests. In all actuality, investors from other countries are still investing in different opportunities. They may be more cautious, but they still have an interest in investing.

6. Another myth is that the older closed in industrial properties are typically obsolete and vacant. In reality, the industrial properties are normally close to the major cities are very desirable for many last mile types of distribution facilities.

7. Another misbelief is that suburban offices are no longer a desire in the industry. This is false. There are many suburban office spaces that are in high demand and it is a very big-ticket property, especially when it is rich in amenities. The needs of the tenant are more modern. They are seeking to bring in the younger type of workforce, so the office spaces that are desired normally are located in urban areas that are rich with culture.

8. Everyone thinks that millennials are the multi-housing future when it comes to demand. This is not true. Seniors, as well as baby boomers, are on the incline of renting apartments. With the amount of student

debt, along with changing lifestyles, home purchasing is delayed. Millennials have been a huge catalyst for the demand on apartments over the past ten years. More and more, millennials are actually taking advantage of apartments, along with the senior population. They do not want to seal with the hidden fees and maintenance of owning their own homes.

PART 1: What You Need to Know Before Acquisition: Here we are going to define all the basics that you need to know as an investor and a landlord.

Chapter 1: Learning the Basics of Commercial Real Estate Investing

It is now time to look over what you need to know in order to be a successful investor with real estate, even if you are just beginning. You will learn at your own speed. Over the course of reading this book you are able to learn how to invest wisely and build your portfolio and your future.

What is Commercial Real Estate Anyway?

Commercial real estate refers to all the properties out there that are retail, industrial, office, warehouse, mixed use, and apartments. There are many different advantages to investing in these and there are many important things you need to consider if you want to become a smart investor.

What does that mean for you as an investor? You will have a steady cash flow, readily available renters, and low risks of vacancy, which will lead you to a very high-income potential. But it is important to ensure that you have done your due diligence and that you know what you need to do in order to ensure that the property will work with your overall strategy.

Step 1: Is Commercial Property Investment Right for You?

The very first thing that you need to decide is if commercial property will be part of your investment plan. You need to make sure that you know how the property is going to meet your goals, as well as your needs. Any property type, whether it is brick and mortar or a home, you can use it to gain income streams. Commercial real estate constitutes as:

- Any retail building.
- Any office space or buildings.
- Warehouses; active or not.
- Industrial type buildings.
- Apartment complexes or duplexes.
- Mixed use type of buildings, where it can serve and retail, apartments, or office spaces.

There are many different nuances with it comes to managing each one of these types of properties. To give you a general picture of what it may look like investing in one of these, let us examine the pros and cons of a single-story retail commercial building, like a strip mall.

The positive reasons why you should invest in a commercial property are as follows:

- There is a tremendous amount of income potential. This is by far the best reason to invest in commercial properties over any residential. The earning potential is much higher. Commercial properties normally have a yearly return off of the purchase price that is between 6-12 percent. This depends on the location of the property, which is also much higher in range than a typical single family type home.

- You will make professional relationship connections. There are small business owners that will take a lot of pride in their business and will want to protect their investments. Owners of the commercial properties are typically not just individuals, but are LLCs. They typically operate the property as their business. This means the landlord and the tenant have much more of a business to customer type relationship, which will help keep the interactions courteous and commercial properties are in the public's eye. The tenants of retail units or buildings will have vested their own interest in the maintenance of the location so that they are able to maintain sales. If they do not, then their sales will go down.

As a result of this, commercial tenants and the owner of the property will have aligned interests. This will help the owner keep maintain, and even improve, the value of their property.

- There are limited hours specified for operations. Businesses typically go home during the night. To paraphrase, you work when they do. This bars the emergency calls that you could have during the night time hours. This includes fire alarms, break ins, and more. You will not get any midnight calls.

- There are more of an objective price evaluation. It is often much easier to evaluate the property price of a commercial property due to being able to request the current owner's statement of income. This will allow you to determine what the price is able to be based on. Should the seller be using a knowledgeable or experienced broker, the price will be set at a specified price in which an investor is able to earn their maximum possible income. Residential type of properties are typically subject to a more emotional type of pricing.

What About Cash Flow?

When you are looking at your cash flow, you need to make sure that you understand all your expectations. You are going to need to ask yourself these questions.

1. If there is a property that has a lower cash flow in a month, is it a good deal?
2. If there is a property that has a higher cash flow, but has other risks, is it a good fit for me?

You are going to need to think about these strategies and from there you are going to need to look at your expectations. You are going to need to look at everything from an unbiased view and ensure that the property is going to work for you. After you have done this, you are going to need to look at the more passive income strategies, as well as what you can do to the property to add value.

What is a Value Add?

When it comes to a value add, you are referring to work that needs to be completed before you can get a higher rent, as well as meet state laws and codes. What that means is that a value-add property is going to meet the following items.

1. It will need renovation.
2. There may be deferred maintenance.
3. The outside of the property may need to be improved or changed.

What you must remember is that the value add will need to be factored into your strategy itself. You will need to think about aspects of renovations when you evaluate a potential property. That will also mean you will need to evaluate the specific property repeatedly. As you move along in the renovations, you will see the worth of the property rise in value.

What is Holding Time?

When you are looking at a certain property it is very important to ensure that you know what the time frame is for the holding time. This means that you will need to know which of the properties that you own are going to be ready to occupy first. Here are a few things that you will need to take a look at when you are looking for a commercial property investment.

a. You want to make sure that you have holding time on the property of one to three years.

b. You need to make sure that you can sell in 12 months if that is going to be a part of your strategy.
c. You should have cash flow properties that are in place to help you to generate income if needed and invest into another property.

What is Appreciation?

When seeking out properties, you will need to keep in mind that you need to know what type of time frame you want to have the properties. For example, you may want to keep an apartment complex for a maximum of ten years, whereas you may only want a certain home for one year in order to sell for a profit. A few questions to ask yourself while you are evaluating them are:

a. Is there a lot of demand for the space?
b. Are people moving to the area more quickly?
c. Have prices gone up or down?
d. Are there lots of businesses that are coming to the area?

These are the kinds of things that you will need to think about when you are determining how long you want to hold onto the property for; however, these will also help you to choose the time that you require for your investment.

Step 2: Decide if Multi Family Investments Are Going to Help You Meet Your Needs and Strategy

When you are pondering jumping into the investing game with a multi-family property, you will want to ensure that you know the type of plan you want to utilize. That will also mean you need to make sure that you are using these properties that are located near schools and other types of residential properties.

What is a Cash Flow Project?

A cash flow project is the net of the cash flow that is associated with a specified project for a year. The calculation is "Sources of the cash - The uses of the cash = The Project Cash Flow". The financial planning will provide a way to show what the cash flow will be for a project or an account. It will provide many choices that is in regards to how the account will affect the flow of cash. A cash flow project includes these features:

a. It will be the main driver for a multi-family property.
b. It will have a high occupancy rate. The residents will renew their leases repeatedly.
c. Units are going to be above the local rental rates.

What is a Value-Add Project?

The phrase value-add is typically used in order to describe a function of a project. Value is a term that is based on how much a buyer would purchase an item for; what it is worth. Project management is a type of service that will add value by offering a lead on a project. This person will deliver the project in specified parameters. In this regard it will be a project that will add value to your property. A value add project will have these features:

a. Lower occupancy rates.
b. Units will be below the rates in the area.
c. Operational costs are going to be very high.
d. The inside or outside may need a facelift.
e. These are going to be harder to manage than a cash flow property.

What is a Hold Period Project?

These are projects that will compare the cash flow to the value of the property. These are the things you need to ask if you have a multifamily property that aligns with the cash flow needs of your strategy.

a. How does the rental fees compare with the rental rates in the market?

b. How is the inside and outside of the property compared to others in the area?
c. What is the occupancy rate and is it high enough for a monthly cash flow?
d. What can be done to make this a better deal? Can I increase the occupancy rates?

Step 3: Decide if Retail/Triple Net Lease is the Right Approach for You.

A triple net lease, or a NNN, refers to the lease when the tenant pays all the taxes, maintenance, and insurance on a property. It also means that the tenant will pay all the fees that are a part of the property for all of the following reasons:

a. It is a less hands on strategy.
b. Returns are lower on this than other investment strategies. This is a more passive approach.
c. The risk is less.
d. These are easy to manage.

The main strategy is also implemented when you want to make sure you have a great portfolio.

Step 4: Understand How Commercial Bank Financing Works

Commercial property financing is done in a different way from residential. Many of the options out there are going to require that the investors have higher net worth standards. That also means that they are going to have to meet a higher and larger commitment.

What About Interest Rates?

The interest rate on the commercial properties will depend on the prime rate. You need to have an understanding on how it is possible to get your money back that you have invested.

a. What is the prime rate? The prime rate is the lowest rate in which the money is able to be borrowed for commercial properties.
b. How do the banks borrow money? Banks borrow at a prime rate, then the banks will loan you the money and add interest to it. This ensures that the bank can pay bank the loan, and make money.

What is Amortization?

Banks will stretch out the amortization period. That means that you might have a 10 year loan with a period of 20 years to pay the loan back. Essentially the amortization, or AM is the period of time that you will have to pay back the loan that was borrowed. This is the debt you will pay on a monthly basis. The shorter the AM is, the higher the total payment will be in each month. There are pros and cons to a short AM.

    a. A longer AM has a lower debt payment, but also has a higher interest payment.

    b. A shorter AM has a higher debt payment, but a lower interest rate.

What is the Length of the Loan?

The length of the loan is dependent on the length of the lease itself. When you are deciding between all the options out there, you want to think about the length of the loan and the amortization period.

What is a Triple Net Lease/Retail Financing?

Triple Net Leases, as well as retailing financing, are typically outlined on the following factors.

    a. The term of the lease will determine the amortization period, as well as the loan period.

b. The down payment will be between 25% - 35%.
c. The interest rate is lower, but will depend on the down payment made and the terms of the lease.
d. Banks will work to refinance when there is a new lease signed. But there may also be an interest rate change that will be higher than the five to six percent rate that is normally granted.

What is Multi-Family Financing?

If you choose to purchase a multi-family home to invest in, there are many kinds of options when it comes to multi-family financing.

a. Agency Lending: This is the kind of financing that occurs for properties that are valued at more than one million dollars. This is the type of loan that has a period of 30 years and a low fixed rate, as well for a short period of time.
b. Traditional Lending: This is the kind of financing that has very specific loan terms. These are usually at a rate of 5 - 6 percent and they may also have a 25-year period of amortization.

What is Single Family Financing versus Commercial Financing?

A single-family home will have all the following conditions:

a. It will be amortized evenly over the whole term of the loan.
b. It will have a higher interest rate throughout the entire loan period.
c. There will be a higher demand and a secondary market that is out there of the single-family homes.
d. It is often based on the appraisal of the home.

Commercial financing typically will explore all the following conditions:

a. The loan term will match the lease period.
b. There will be a longer amortization period.
c. There will be an interest rate that is for a set period, then there will be a floating period.
d. There is a smaller secondary market that has been created to ensure that there is going to be a higher value.
e. The loan will be based on the cash flow of the property and not on the value.

There are five different types of commercial real estate loans. These types of loans are normally used to purchase or renovate a commercial property. An owner occupied property is typically considered to one where the business is already occupied at least 51 percent of the building. These types of mortgages are typically used to finance commercial buildings and mixed use buildings. It is also used for office buildings and retail type centers.

1. SBA 7 Loan: This is a loan for someone established in business that is looking for a long term loan. It is normally owner occupied property. The loan goes up to $5,000,000.00. You will have to be in business for at least 2 years. The loan is normally done for 25 years. The time to fund is 60 to 90 days.

2. CDC / SBA 504 Loan: This is for established businesses that are looking for a long term loan. This is for an owner occupied commercial load. The loan amount is up to 90 percent of the total purchase price of the property. The term is 10 - 20 years long. The time of funding is 60 to 90 days.

3. Traditional Mortgages: This is for businesses that are looking for a long term type of loan where the property is owner occupied. The business owner will need to have amazing credit in order to get one of

these loans. Typically, the borrower will need to have a credit score of about 700 plus. The loan amount will cover up to 85 percent of the total purchase price. The term of the loan is 7 - 30 years. The time of funding ranges from 30 - 90 days.

Step 5: You Need to Know How to Read a Commercial Rental Property Proforma

A commercial rental proforma is going to be a complete financial analysis of a property. It is a statement that will allow you to know the revenue, the vacancy, and the operating expenses.

What is the Gross Revenue?

The gross revenue is the maximum amount that you are able to to get from the property if everything is occupied by tenants.

What is a Vacancy?

This is the percentage of the gross revenue. it is calculated by looking at the projects vacancy rates. Many investors are able to do this by creating a financial model that is based on five percent less than the rate of occupancy.

What are Operating Expenses?

The operating expenses are going to include utilities, maintenance, property taxes, as well as your management fees. You need to keep in mind that the triple net lease property will not pay you the operating expenses.

Multi-family properties should see about a 25% to 40% of the gross revenue that will be dedicated to operating expenses. The latter number will depend on a lot of different things, including the way that the property is classified. For example, if it is a cashflow or value add property. If it is going to be the latter, you are going to need to keep the property and the upgrade costs in mind when you are thinking about the expenses.

What is Debt Service?

The debt service is the portion that you require in order to pay your debt payment. That is without all of the operating costs out there.

What is NOI?

Net Operating Income, also known as NOI, is the equivalence of:

Gross Revenue - Vacancy - Operating Expenses

The NOI is calculated as the cash that you get before all of the taxes have come out. However, after you have paid all of the calculated expenses, it does not have anything to do with the debt service.

What is COC?

COC stands for "cash on cash". This is the ROI after you have taken out the debt service amount. It is crucial that you ensure the COC is not calculated on the price of the purchase. Instead it needs to be on the down payment that you are using to purchase the commercial investment property.

What is the Internal Rate of Return?

The IRR looks at how an investment is performing as it calculates the number by showing the total value of money that is made in the property investment. Then it is compared to another investment. The IRR helps you to see if your investment is growing in the right way. It will also show you if there is another investment opportunity that will lead you to a better IRR.

Step 6: Understanding the Triple Net Lease

As discussed earlier, there are many commercial real estate investors who want to have a lower rick, as well as a passive strategy that will allow you to have other opportunities that are going to exist with the triple net. It is crucial to make sure that you are aware and understand this before you move in this direction.

What is an Absolute Triple Net (NNN)?

When you are in an Absolute NNN, it will follow these basic principles:

a. You will own the building, but all the expenses are going to be paid by the tenant.
b. Property taxes, maintenance, and insurance are paid by the tenant.
c. The expenses, the fees, the rent and more are going to be written into the lease. In addition to this, it will be determined how the tenant will pay the expenses. Will they be paid directly to the tenant or to the landlord?

What is a NN (Double Net)?

In an NN here is how it normally works.

a. The expenses are all billed to the tenant except for the parking, as well as the roof.
b. There are expenses that are associated with the roof and those will sometimes be an expense that will last over 20 to 30 years depending on the terms of the lease.
c. The structure of the lease can vary when the building is going up and will change depending on the way that it is built. That will mean either lower or higher expenses to the owner.

What are Lease Terms?

When it comes to the terms of a lease, it is important to keep these things in mind:

a. If the lease is going to be three years or less, you want to make sure that you have an 8% CAP or higher. The reason for this cap is that you are going to have a higher risk when you have a shorter term.
b. If the lease term is 3 to 5 years, you want to make sure you have a 7 - 8% CAP.
c. If the lease is going to be 10 years or more, you want a 7% CAP.

What About Comps in the Area for Both Rent and Sales?

When you are looking into the other potential areas, it is important to look at the following criteria:

a. Look at the rent prices, as well as the terms for other buildings that are in the same area.
b. Make sure that you look at what the tenant is paying for rent.
c. What are the recent sales as they are happening in the area?
d. What is the CAP for similar buildings that have sold in the area?
e. What is the Grade of the Tenant?

When you are evaluating the tenant, you must look at the following aspects:

a. What is their creditworthiness?
b. Is this tenant trustworthy?
c. Are they backed by a public company?

In general, the better the grade of the tenant, the lower the CAP will be. But if the CAP is lower, then there are going to be higher rade tenants that are going to be lower risk than your existing tenants.

The role of the property management company is to ensure that they can work and assist you with the management of assets. How much you are expecting out of the manager will also influence how much they are going to be paid. If there is a hands off approach there is going to be a much higher cost for the manager.

Step 8: Decide if Asset Management is Needed

Investor assurance will be given to you by an industry expert, not the affiliates, but by others who are working to explore all the market opportunities that are out there.

     a. Some commercial investments will offer asset management opportunities as well. This is a passive investment approach.

     b. You will have the knowledge of being able to see local experts on the ground floor who will be able to assist with input and assure that you are able to share your expertise with your investment.

     c. You want to use the knowledge of an experienced investor when you are looking at all this information.

How Do I Know When I Should Use an Asset Manager?

You will use an asset manager when you are buying a multi-tenant property, that means that you are going to be able to enjoy a property that has many different units financed. In this situation the location is going to be more complex. You are going to want to have the ideas of the asset managers so they can guide you through the entire process.

Chapter 2: Bootstrapping and Doing the Grind

One of the first questions that you must ask yourself is why you want to go into commercial real estate. The reason for that is it must be a fundamental principle that will guide you in all your decisions. The reason that every person says that they want to go into real estate is money. Some people always wonder if you make more money in commercial or residential. It is important to look at the example below.

Here are a few sample transactions.

A Sample Residential Transaction:

Agent sells a home for $275,000.00

Agent has a brokerage with another firm and the list is from the other firm.

The agent's firm will get 3%.

The agent will get 65% of the sale from the firm

The total commission for the agent is $5,362.50

A Sample Commercial Transaction:

An agent leases a 7,500 square foot of space at 3 years and $12.00 per square foot.

Agents and co-brokers work with another firm.

The agent's firm will get 3%.

The agent will get a 65% commission, if you were selling a $50,000,000 mall what would be your commission? It is likely that there will not be any time for you to be doing those transactions any time soon. There are many cases where you can make a lot of money if you are willing to work on putting together these kinds of deals.

While there are many transactions that will close on the residential side in about one to two months of the contract, there are commercial deals that do not. Even when there is a 7,500 square foot lease that has been handled for a long time and it is done and paid, the transaction could also close in a few weeks.

The shopping center that we outlined above shows that while it can be hard and frustrating, but it also can be very satisfying when things are going right for you. One of the other advantages to the field is the variety of it.

What Are My Career Options?

For many years after comparing the two, I decided to investigate all the options that are out there for someone who is in commercial real estate.

What is General Brokerage?

These are commercial agents that can represent either buyers or sellers, they are going to be a part of every step of the process. These are agents that are normally contractors and not direct employees of any company. The reason for that is they work solely on commission. They can look at the market and they are able to adapt to the needs that are outlined. They are able to specialize in all the product types out there. They may specifically be a part of a region or a kind of real estate.

What is Development?

There are many areas that an agent can work, and some of those include being a part of development itself. Also, that can be something like project management and leasing. When there is development staff, they work to make sure that something is getting built on the land. Whether that is going to be a shopping center, or it is going to be an office building.

The developer will arrange all the financing and from there they will work on the anchor of the leases. They are also going to hire architects and the contractors. They will also ensure that they can be a part of the process until all the tenants move in.

What is Property Management?

When a property is being built or when it is being developed, it needs to be managed. This happens when there is a property manager that is handling all the parts of the property. That means that they are handling the staffing, contracting, repairs and more. They are also being employed by the firms and will be paid a salary.

What Can I Expect?

All of what you can expect is different based on where you are and what you are selling. Here are some figures that were outlined in 2006 from a survey of the National Association of Realtors.

1. Over half of all respondents had an income of $75,000 to $249,000, and about 5% of

them had an income of over $500,000 USD or more.

2. Selling commercial real estate generated a huge profit over leasing as more than half reported a volume of 2 million dollars or above.

3. Half of these people have been involved in real estate for over 16 years.

4. Most of them work exclusively in commercial real estate. There are 25% who are newer who have a mix of commercial and residential.

What Are My First Steps?

If you are considering a change in careers you need to think about what you are going to do to ensure that you are on the right path. Here is what you should do:

- Step 1: List all the people that you know in commercial real estate.
- Step 2: Call of your friends and relatives and see who they know in commercial real estate.
- Step 3: Start calling. Then ask those that are in the business to give you some time and ensure that you are not seeking a position at the time.

- Step 4: Conduct an interview, ask them how they got started and what advice they would want to give to someone who was new. You are going to want to make sure that you have a few ideas of people that you should talk to and what you need to expect.
- Step 5: Ensure that you narrow down your search to all the important aspects. Look at sites that are specific to real estate and look at all the jargon and important information.
- Step 6: Ensure that you know all the details that are out there about employment. You need to know the compensation structure and make sure that you know everything to expect.
- Step 7: Go through the interview process. You need to be ready for the process. Look at all your choices and ensure you have it narrowed down to just five. You are going to want to ensure that you are making the right choice.
- Step 8: After you have landed the job, you are going to want to call back your person of contact for another meeting and then talk to them about valuable lessons. You do not want to spend too much time talking about your wants and needs. You want to hear all that they have to say.

How Can I Kickstart My Career in Commercial Real Estate?

When you are getting started in commercial real estate you need to remember that everyone started where you are right now. It is important to ensure that you are taking all the first steps into the industry in a way that you will be comfortable and in a way that will allow you to know you have made the right choices.

1. Sign up for local classes: You want to make sure that you are educating yourself as much as possible to ensure that you know all you can. In addition to this, you want to ensure that you are networking with other people who are in the business.

2. Read all you can get your hands on: You want to find everything that you can on commercial real estate. You are going to need to find the best people that are in the business, as well and learn from them. That is going to help you to start taking real action. Education is key.

3. Go to local meet ups and seminars in your area: One thing that will help you to be very successful is to attend as many events as you can. You need to be as knowledgeable as possible on the ways things are work in

the business. You want to look at all the meetups that are out there and attend as many classes as you can. Also get out and meet as many people as you can in your field.

4. Become an intern at a local firm: if you want to ensure that you are going to have a great hands on experience, you need to learn from a local agent. Everyone wants help and that means that you are not going to need a college degree. You want to call and request a meeting in order to get all the balls rolling.

5. Find Your Specific Niche: You need to know what you are interested in. If you are looking at retail, offices, hotels or what you are going to see that these are all niches. You want to find your sweet spot, and then use it to your advantage.

6. Have Memberships: You are going to want to check out the ICSC and ensure that you know what you need to do if you are involved in retail. You want to make sure that you are looking at all the associations that you are going to be a part of, and then you can set up lots of local meetings. This will allow you to be a part of the restaurant.

7. Have People Write Letters: You want to let people write letters and you want to always congratulate them on new projects. You

want to ensure that you are following a five second rule.

8. Read Important Trade Magazines: You want to make sure that you are on top of the markets and that you know what is happening with all the columns and the publications out there.

9. Follow People and Companies on Social Media: Make sure that you are following everything that the individuals are doing, and you want to ensure that you can share their content. You will see what other companies are in the news for, as well as staying up to date. You want to make sure that you are taking at least 30 minutes a day and you are educating yourself on everything that is happening in the industry.

10. Join Your Local Chamber of Commerce: Take the time to join your local chamber of commerce and be an important part of the community.

Chapter 3: Utilizing Your Knowledge of Areas Near You

Anytime that you are considering a swap in careers or are looking for new information, you need to know how to take advantage of local resources.

1. **Local Colleges**: When it comes to learning as easily as possible there are many local colleges that will have courses on commercial real estate. Most of the time these courses are taught by experienced commercial real estate professionals. They can help you with the process of learning, how to get started, as well as what path to choose in your career. You should take the time to check with a local school to make sure that you are choosing the right course. You may be able to take the class, as well as an audit which will offer you a lower tuition if there is a cost at all. You need to check with the local school to see how this works.

2. **Take an Online Course:** One of the best benefits of technology is the fact that there are many online courses out there that will

help you with the process of learning the commercial real estate business. One of the best ways to be successful with this is to find one of the most popular courses from a site or association that has been around for a long time. One such example is Discovering Commercial Real Estate by the National Association of Realtors. This course is delivered completely online. It points out all the differences that are out there for commercial as well as residential real estate. Students who are a part of the class will be able to know and explain the role of the broker and decide all the different kinds of properties, understanding the valuation methods, and looking at many other resources.

3. This is not a course that is going to equip an agent, but it is a course that will help a person decide if it is the right path for them and to understand it all. The course is perfect for an agent who is recently licensed or for someone who wants to learn more.

4. **Read All of the Industry Publications**: Commercial trade journals are one of the best ways to ensure that you are on top of

information that is out there about the market and to stay ahead of your competition. There are many resources that are out there that will help you to stay connected. There are many though that have the hyper focus that you are bound to find when you're looking at trade publications specifically. You need to ensure that you can tap into the list of potential clients and partners that you are able to have when you are advertising. A part of that is using written submissions that help to drive your brand awareness. You want to ensure that you are bringing continual excellent prospects to your business. Here is a complete list of all the trade journals that you are going to want to follow if you are a part of the business.

a. **BOMA or Building Owners and Managers Association International:** This is the main source of information when you are talking about building development, leasing, development, and more. There are many options out there as well for you to look at for legislation. It will also show you the occupancy numbers to know about all the developments. BOMA is the number one source for being able to keep up with all the trends and the changes in regulation. You can find more info here: http://stamatscorp.com/boma/2018_ BOMA_MediaPlanner.pdf

b. **CCIM:** The CCIM is a commercial real estate professional organization that shares educational information through its program. It is led by the practitioners of the institute and this is the most prestigious certification of the entire industry. CCIM published two times a month and it is mailed to all subscribers. More information can be found on the CCIM website.

c. **NAIOP:** This is the Commercial Real Estate Development Association, which is a group for developers, owners, and professionals in the industry. This is a magazine that serves as a location to ensure that the information for the industry for all commercial real estate professionals. This is a publication that comes out every quarter and it is one that is full of news and columns. More information can be found here: https://www.naiop.org/en/Sponsor-and-Advertise/Print-Advertising.aspx

5. **Meetup Groups:** One of the best things you can do is join local meet up groups and virtual groups. You want to start your search on LinkedIn. Do not get worried if there are some that are out of your area. Many of the best groups these days can be virtual. You can also find other associations that will allow you to network and meet new people.

Chapter 4: Finding the Best Areas

When it comes to investing in commercial real estate it is very well documented that it will help you to diversify your portfolio. However, in addition to that it is going to help you to generate cash flow and to have a real appreciation in value over time. There are many properties that generate income. These are mainly going to be commercial, as well as a multi family homes. These are huge investments for all strategies and to ensure that you can buy what is the most important and invest your dollars wisely. One thing that is very clear is that not all markets are equal.

Where are the Best Places to Invest Anyway?

Commercial and other markets are always changing so it is important to make sure that you are looking at and are weighing the value of your investment on a regular basis. When you are going you need to ensure you have a portfolio that is perfect for you as an investor. It is one that is going to help you always rely on in the same way that you would want to have a reliable investment opportunity you need to think about the way that all the economic indicators are going to help you get great returns.

What is the Discounted Cash Flow Analysis Model?

Discounted Cash Flow Analysis, which is also known as DCF, is the method that is used to ensure value in all assets. This is specifically helpful when it comes to commercial real estate. The way it works is rather simple. The value of the dollar now is worth more than the value of the dollar in the future. The value of the asset is the sum of all the future cash flows and the way that they are then discounted for risk.

When it comes to the method of timing all the cash flows, it is important to look at the price that an investor would be willing to pay on an asset now. When there are riskier cash flow streams that are out there, they are going to require that they are discounted at even higher rates. That means that there is going to be a chance of an income stream and 100% chance of recurring in the future value. It is important that the analysis happens for the investor.

Real estate investors need to be familiar and come up with a way to look at the capitalization rates that are a short cut for real assets to be looked at. DCF is a way to look at the total value of an asset.

When looking at the value we are going to look at how to value it without any kind of leverage. What that means is that they need to be evaluated on a regular basis without looking at all the risk factors. One of the largest mistakes that is made based on investors is looking at the leveraged return and then ignoring all the other components. An investment that is looking at a 15% return would use a 60% leverage, and then would be less risk than one that had a 20% return, and a 90% leverage. It is important to make sure that you are looking at the value.

In order to know and determine the value, it would be important to look at all the value and then to calculate the total worth today. When it comes to a discount rate it is simply required to know what the level of risk is assumed. The important thing you must understand is that the lower the discount rates are when they are applied to investments, the lower risk characteristics and higher rates are applied to other projects that have higher risk characteristics.

How is a Property's Cash Flow Determined Anyway?

The cash flow is determined by adding in the annual cash flow, as well as the sales and proceeds. That will be known as the residual value. This value is calculated by looking at the income in the course of a year and then looking at it and dividing it by the future capitalization rate. The rate does not tell the whole story and there is a balance that happens. This is a part of all the other factors.

Fundamentals You Must Weigh for a Good Analysis

Every single city that is out there is known by its own drivers and its own indicators. There are many things that are being tracked out there by many government entities, such as the Census Bureau and Labor statistics. There are also many real estate think tanks out there that publish other numbers you need to know, and they sell the subscriptions for their data markets.

Data alone is not enough; you need to look at all the numbers and information out there. You need to look at all the factors that are going to help you to make a great investment in a formula. This will help you to invest and remove bias when you are looking at the analysis. The main result in looking at all of these is that you need to look at the foundation out there in order to make better choices.

How to Develop an Objective Model

When looking at all the models and the indicators the most important ones are the ones that drive the data and the potentiality of future profitability. Here are the ones you need to watch and where you can find the numbers.

1. The Population Growth: The Census Bureau changes from year to year. The growth in an area will drive all the demand for real estate. When it comes to multifamily properties there is a rising population that ensures that there is a large growing population. Recently, the census showed the greatest 5-year millennial gain was in Colorado Springs, Colorado.

2. The Job Market: The Bureau of Labor Statistics looks at the biggest gains in the workforce in some cities like Orlando, Seattle and Houston. Orlando has the highest 5-year projection of growth of any city in the USA.

3. The Cost of Business: The ease of starting a company is also very important when it comes to the factors like taxes, energy, and credit. When it comes to the fastest growing cities, Seattle has the largest wage growth in 2017 with 7.52%.

4. The Industry Concentration: Investors are weighing the prospects for things like medical offices. They are wanting to think about things like the healthcare employment pool. When looking at the annual survey it is important to look at all the options out there from consulting firms. Firms such as PWC, are helpful about assisting with the health and education jobs. They make sure that they are looking at the numbers.

5. The Housing Affordability: One of the largest issues with dealing with many cities that are gateway cities like New York, Los Angeles, and San Francisco is the cost of housing. There are many other groups that compare the local incomes. San Francisco always has the least favorable market out there and for that reason it has required an income of at least $119,000 just to live there. Chicago's affordability also has been something that has attracted investors for many years.

6. The Sentiments of Investors and the People: There are many surveys out there that have looked at the interest of the investors, as well as the interest of other people in the areas of Dallas, Brooklyn, Orlando, and Nashville. These are the areas that are

booming the most in the USA. This also looks at the lifestyle and the demographic as far as the education of the areas. One of the best areas for companies choosing to relocate seems to be the Chicago area. There are many areas that are known for their work life balance and other factors.

7. The Capitalization Rates: When it comes to finding good properties, it is important to look at what investors become fixated on and see that there are many options when it comes to cap rates. This is the amount of income that can be generated by the first year of ownership and by looking at all the expenses after the debt cost. What that also means is that it is important to look at all the year to year movements. That is going to show you what is volatile, as well as what can be changed. There is so much risk that happens over a long period.

8. The Growth of Rent: It is also important to look at the ways that rent has increased over the past few years as well. When rent is continuing to go up in an area it is an indicator that the value of the property will continue to rise. That will always mean good things in the long term for your investment.

Chapter 5: Utilizing Your Knowledge of Areas Near You

When you live in a local area, you have an advantage over a person who is trying to break in from another location. When your area is your home you have seen the patterns in growth, and you have watched over the years as the area has developed. It is this very development that will always lead you to having a real advantage over someone who is trying to come that is part of an outside market. Let's look together at a few things that are going to help you to stay ahead of the curve when you are looking at the local area.

How to Become a Local Expert

One of the most important things is to make sure that you are networking with those around you. They will tell you when there are exciting projects that are coming up, even before you have started to watch the building construction. What this means is that there are so many ways to communicate and connect. Here is what you can do.

Connect on LinkedIn with Local Influencers

When it comes to making sure that you find out about all the trends in your area, you want to know that you are connecting to the local influencers. There are people in your area that have more power than you know. That power is due to their knowledge of things that are going on in their niche. For example, a local tech manager may be able to tell you about a new office park that is about to open. A local restaurant owner may be able to tell you about a new mall where he is going to have a location. Having your fingers on the pulse and the word of mouth of the community is a face to face and a virtual process. How can it be done virtually? The fastest way is to connect on LinkedIn. Let's start at the beginning.

What is LinkedIn?

LinkedIn is the largest professional network in the entire world for working professionals who want to connect in an online platform and make meaningful relationships for business online. There are over 270 million professionals who are currently on the platform and they are from over 180 countries across the world. You can meet people from any region and any background on LinkedIn. So, the first thing to do is to make sure that you have created a LinkedIn profile and that you have listed your experience, as well as set yourself up on the network as a local commercial real estate investor.

People generally now think of LinkedIn as a virtual business card. What that means to you is that you want to make sure you go to the site to create a profile with all your experience with your background.

What if I am New to the Commercial Real Estate Business and I Feel Like I Do Not Have Enough Experience?

First, it is important to remember that everyone started somewhere and a part of that starting somewhere is making sure that you have a profile that reflects that you are new. You should go to the site and fill out all your past job experience. Take the time and explain that you are new to the commercial real estate world in the Summary section.

This area allows you to share your experience and to reach out to new people who are looking to connect with professionals like you. Ninety percent of the results that are going to help the people looking on the site are going to come back from two places. The text that you put in the summary section and the keywords that you add as well to the bottom of your profile. For this reason, it is important to make sure that you have thought about these areas the most on that profile.

What Do You Mean by Profile Keywords?

LinkedIn has a skills section in the bottom of the profile where you fill in all your relevant skills to the position you have had. You will want to take your time and make up a long list of keywords that suit the jobs you have had in the past. You will want to create a list of at least 25 skills as this is the basis for the people who will want to connect with you. List your most relevant skills to your current position first. That will always get the highest amount of attention.

How Do Professionals Find Me?

When it comes to LinkedIn professionals, they can find you from the search page. When they are looking to connect, they are going to enter in an area and what they are looking for. LinkedIn is almost like an Amazon for people and jobs. People can connect with other professionals who are similar if they are in need of those skills. Someone may be looking for a professional like you to connect with and have a friend with the same kind of expertise that you provide.

Should I Get a Premium LinkedIn Account?

It is worth taking the time to get a premium LinkedIn account because when you have one you can connect with any number of professionals you want to quickly and easily.

There is no limit to the number of professionals that you can connect with on the network from just the perspective of it being a premium or free account. However, there is a limit to the number of InMail's that you can send out as a free account or as a premium account. There are different tiers of membership. The basic premium account will give you access to 200 InMail's per month. There are some people who have their email addresses on their profiles; however, there are other professionals who prefer their email addresses hidden. Those professionals can only be accessed through InMail. What this means is that in order to connect with them you are going to need to have a premium account.

How Much is a LinkedIn Premium Account?

Generally, they are about $75.00 per month; however, you can also get more InMail's in a month if you do not want to upgrade your membership after this threshold. That will ensure that you can connect with the professionals that you want to in a method that is effective. So, your next question may be then, how many connections do I want to make a month? As an effective influencer who is trying to have a process as well as a method. You need to be reaching out to 1,000 professionals a month. The maximum number of connections though that you can have on LinkedIn is 5000 for an account. After that 5000 thresholds, people must follow you. In following you, they are still able to see all you post and mail you. But there is a threshold limit in the same way that there is for Facebook.

How Do I Connect With 1000 People a Month?

There are many ways to connect with a thousand people a month. The first thing that you need to do is decide who you want to connect with, and then create search parameters that are going to bring you back the number of people that you need. So, let's look at this a bit more. As referenced earlier, when you are looking at the search parameters, you can look for someone by keyword, area, or by industry. You are best served to have someone in every single area that is going to be able to help you keep your pulse on the industry, as well as on the area. That person will function as an expert for the industry or the area on all things that will happen. As a successful professional you need to have your own expert panel. You can think of your connections as your own expert panel. Here is what you need to do:

1. Create a list of industries: Make sure you are covering every vertical. This can be very general like tech, restaurants, etc.
2. Make a list of areas you want to cover: This is all the cities that are a part of your metro area that you might want to make investments in.
3. Have a list of the skills of these professionals: Project Management, City Planning etc. These are some of the general skills you would want to plan out.
4. From there make a list of job titles: If you are not sure by certain industries what the title would be, you can use keywords for this same function.

Now I Have a List: What Am I Creating?

What you are creating here is your own expert panel. That panel is going to allow you to then connect with your intended verticals and make sure that you are making the right connections. A thing to consider though is that you want to look at the profile of the person and see how active they are. Some people are more active on social media platforms like LinkedIn because they are actively looking to connect with other professionals who they might be able to really build a network with. There are other professionals though that are only on LinkedIn because it is the expectation that anyone who wants to have a career is there now a days. The way to see how active they are is to also look at the last timing of their last post. People have the ability in the same way that they can post on Facebook to post on LinkedIn. It is that posting ability that allows professionals to share things that they are passionate. There are some professionals who are very serious about their network that will accept your connection right off the bat and work with you to build meaningful connections.

Should I Get Sales Navigator?

Depending on how much time you have or do not have, you may want to go ahead and sign up for Sales Navigator. So, what is it? It is an application that allows you to sign up for a quick and affordable solution that will allow you to track, as well as to look at all your connections and connection leads in one place. If you are a real estate agent or you are looking to become one, this is a great way to follow all your prospects and look at all the details of your interactions with them. Sales Navigator helps you to look for people as well as to connect with them. In addition to that, you can also add all kinds of templates that are perfect for you to be able to send out a lot of connections and business queries quickly.

If you are curious how much something like this costs, it is quite affordable as you can do Sales Navigator for about $150.00 per month. If you are a part of a company, you can get an affordable rate and you can get a discount for more users. You are going to want to spend the time that is required to work with as many professionals as possible when you are signing this deal. Work with them in order to ensure that you are getting the best deal. LinkedIn will be happy to speak with you and your group and go over all the best pricing options for you. To learn more about Sales Navigator check out all of the options listed on the link. You will be amazed at the savings that you can get when you work in a group.

There is also an option for a one month free trial if you are interested. It will assist and help you with the process of being successful. It will aid you in learning if the tool is good for your business model. The tool is very easy to use and is a plug in that just works as a part of your normal UI for LinkedIn.

How Can I Send Out All of These Messages?

One thing that is important to think about is that generating connection leads is a part of the entire process of networking and selling. What that means is that you need to consider what you have in terms of time and find the way to ensure that you can connect in a meaningful way. What does this mean, you are going to need to look at your schedule and determine if you can spend about 20% of your time prospecting. If the answer to that is no, you are going to need to look at how you can use technology to assist you with this process.

There are applications that link into Sales Navigator as well as into the LinkedIn platform. They will help you with the process of being able to automate your messages to people so that you have a template that you will be able to send the information out to. So, the next question you need to ask yourself is why you are reaching out to people. If you are going to use tech, and you are reaching out to make sales and to connect with people, you need at minimum two kinds of templates for messages.

1. A Connection Opportunity: This is an opportunity to make introductions and to share knowledge.

2. A Sales Opportunity: This is an opportunity to make a sale.

The templates will ensure that your message seems very personal even though it is a reach out using a template. When people connect with you, you can then reach out and start a personalized dialogue. Sometimes that is as simple as meeting for a coffee and then discussing the things that you are all wanting to do together and seeing how you can work as a team.

Meeting Connections and Learning in the Physical World

One of the best ways to ensure that you can meet people face to face is by joining a local group like the local Chamber of commerce. That means however, that you should think about looking into all the groups that you should be a part of in your local area. So, if you are in a large city that would mean all the chambers for the metro area. By doing so, you will be on the top of all the changes that are happening in the business. Other things you should consider include signing up for local newsletters so that you will be in the loop of all the construction that is coming in the area.

Part of the best process for all of this is also attending all the local meetings so that you will be able to make those meaningful connections, one at a time.

Make Connections on Meetups and In LinkedIn Groups

If you are looking to meet up with people and discuss things in your area, you can also make and meet in groups on LinkedIn and in Meetups. LinkedIn groups are out there and are sometimes just groups in which people make connections. In others, they are discussing information and meet up to make real life connections. It does not have to be something formal; it can be one time a month when everyone meets and when you are going to discuss a certain topic.

What if I Cannot Find a Group I Want?

If you cannot find the group that you need and want, you need to create the group. You can do that easily when you are ready to make a new group in the application. Make sure that you share with your network so that you have started a new group. When you do this, you will be assured to have more people join you and share their knowledge.

Chapter 6: Choosing the Right Properties

When it comes to finding the best places in your local area, you need to think about what you know around you that is great and where you want to expand to. That means that you should think about what areas are growing, as well as areas that are going through a revitalization. Here are a few pointers for finding the best areas. Here are a few suggestions to help you come up with some good areas to look at.

1. Research areas that are up and coming: There are many things that make an area up and coming. If there has been a large turnover in the ownership of an area and there has been a lot of reinvestment in an area, this makes it up and coming.

2. A lot of new real estate is being added to the area: When an area starts building a lot of apartments and shopping centers, the area is about to undergo a transformation. That means that it is about to have a lot of growth that will improve the quality of life and the amount of money that is flowing into that area.

3. New rail and transit systems are being added: One thing to look at is if there is going to be a new transit system that has been added to an area. That means there is going to be a large increase in the rents, as well as in the values of the homes.

4. Look for rising rental rates: A value of an investment can only go up when there is new multi-tenant buildings that are being added and there is a rent rise. What this also means is that there are new people coming into the area.

5. Follow the local entrepreneurs: You should also look into the styles of the local influencers who are helping to drive the vibe of the community. When there is a younger group that will come in, they will always use their skills to reinvest in the area. There are many new groups that will continue to also invest in the community and help with growth, as well as with a broadening of the way that people look and think about the location.

6. Knowing local demographics: Pay attention to the favorable changes in demographics in an area. One of the best things to look for is an injection of younger blood. These include students coming to an area as well as young professionals who will also

reinvest back into the community. They will be active members. These are people who want to live and work downtown.

7. Priorities of areas are defined by the jobs and the schools in the area. What this means is that there are many people who base where they are planning on living completely according to the closeness of their home and their school. It is important to look at where the schools have the best reputations and how close most people are to their jobs. There are some areas where driving long distances is normal like in LA and Atlanta.

8. Watching for the big box stores: There are some businesses like the Walmart's of the world that are very good indicators that when they appear, they are going to mean their significant opportunity for there to be long term growth. They work with advisors who do a lot of research into a phenomenon before they are willing to come the area.

9. Look at the Spillover Areas: It is important to make sure that you are paying attention to all the areas that are outside of the area that is so hot. When you do this, you will be able to see all the other areas that are continuing to grow and prosper. These are the areas that are just outside of the area that

are going to be there for you to be able to choose from and to choose the best option.

10. Looking at Current Data: When you are investing and you want to make sure that threw are going to be great gains, it is important to look at the data of all of the multifamily units that have been there for at least 120 days or less. That means that you want to look at the return value of at least 70%.

11. Look at the Millennial Areas: One thing that is important to look at is that there are many areas out there that are starting to pop up that are being referred to as Malignifying. These are areas that have many education centers as well as multipurpose shopping centers.

12. Look for Starbucks: When things are going well, it is important to make sure that they are doing well. You are going to want to look at the places like Starbucks so that it is possible to see how an area is doing. When there are multiple locations that are being added, it is possible to know what to expect every time.

Chapter 7: Appraising Properties

When it comes to the method of evaluating commercial property, there is a process that must be used for valuation. The method is done with appraisals in the form of mortgages, sales, mergers, taxation and many other appraisals that are done by property evaluators. Property valuation can be achieved through any of the following techniques:

1. The Cost Method
2. The Comparison of Sales Method
3. The Income Capitalization Approach

The Cost Method is a system which takes the value of the commercial options and then looks at the relevant cost that is currently on the market to construct the property afterwards. The buyer does not pay anything other than the cost that was used to build the property. All the future profit is not accounted for at all in this method.

The Comparison of Sales Method is the way that people can look at similar properties. All the properties are then compared in the methods of sales and the market value. The property value is then looked at in comparison to other properties. All the properties currently on the market which are looked at by the comparison method will be properties that have a lot of similarities. They do not need to be anywhere close to identical, they just need to have many of the same general features in order to be compared in this way.

The Income Capitalization Approach is a method that looks at how you can value a commercial property, which means that the value is the same as the cash flow that will provide more income in the future. The property also has a negative relationship with the current value as well as with all the risk that is used in getting the cash flow. It is important to make sure that you are looking at the available nature of the property to generate cash flow. The other most important part of all the analysis is that you must include in the process the returns on all the investments.

When you are working with an appraiser, they can choose one or more of the above methods in order to properly appraise a property. This means it is possible to make sure that there are many methods that have been outlined in a way so that there is a combination of accurate analysis and demand. It is important to ensure you have the right methods for valuation. Also, you want to make sure that you are working with a professional who can take you through all these details.

How to Learn How to Appraise Commercial Properties: The Basics

The first thing that is important to note is that many people feel overwhelmed when it comes to the idea of a commercial real estate appraisal. It is important to make sure that you are not overwhelmed. You should also look at and understand the process of how it all works before you jump right in. So, here are the basic outlines for why and what happens with a commercial real estate appraisal.

What is the Reason for a Commercial Real Estate Appraisal?

The reason an appraisal is necessary is because it is a part of the valuation of the process for all kinds of commercial real estates. It happens so that you are going to be able to properly know the value of property as it is being sold. This will allow you to figure out what you can do with the property and how much you can get out of real estate, a sale, or another transaction.

Who Conducts the Commercial Real Estate Appraisal?

When it comes to the appraisal it has to be done by a professional. You can think of the person who does the appraisal as a professional real estate detective. He or she will look at all the information that is out there about the property and from there they will be able to make some analysis and conduct some math to get a good idea of what the property is worth.

There are many kinds of commercial appraisals that are happening all the time. An appraiser will have to pass a test and become state certified before they are able to be a part of the appraisal institute. There is a very strict code of ethics and standards that must be followed.

What Events Do You Need Appraisals For?

This list is endless, but these are the basic reasons.

1. You need to determine the price of a property in order to sell.
2. You need to understand the value of the property and how much it will cost.
3. You need it to negotiate the details of a lease and how much you can charge for rent.

4. Appraisals are required for taxes and for assessments.
5. You need it to understand the process of businesses breaking up.
6. An appraisal can help with mergers of companies, stock and other transactions.
7. You need property appraisal for the process of government acquisition.
8. Appraisals are vital for the process of damages valuation or other related issues.
9. You may need it to determine will issues.
10. A general understanding of the process can be helpful for auction proceedings.
11. You may be counseling a client on investments or other issues.

What is the Overall Process for Conducting an Appraisal?

The overall process can vary a lot from one location to another and from one process to another. The structure of the process is pretty much the same across the board generally. It is important to make sure that you know the conditions, features, and the information about the property. It will allow you to have all the details that are relevant to the basic parts of the outline and the structure. You also need to make sure that you have gotten data that is collected from good sources, which means that you are looking at the neighborhood, the property information, and also taking all of the factors into your thoughts such as the utility, scarcity, and the purchasing power of the area. After you have outlined all of this, you are going to find out the values of the appraisal report. The entire process can take a few days to a few weeks and it depends on the location, as well as all the factors that are a part of the request.

What are the Kinds of Reports That Can Come from an Appraisal?

When it comes to the appraisal reports out there, there are many that can cover and determine many factors. It is important to look at the analysis out to allow you to look at the property and the valuation of the property. You will see what you may be risking, as well as things you may encounter. It may have negative impacts on your property valuation.

You need to look at the values and the requirements of all the projects and the clients. There are going to be different standards to the report that are going to be driven by the project and the standards used.

1. Self-Contained Reports: This is a report that looks at all the data that was used and then creates an appraisal across all the areas.
2. Summary Report: This takes all the data and creates an assignment out of all the data. There are many ways that you can look at the other options outside of the report.
3. Restricted Use Report: This is one that has conclusions that are a part of the appraisal. That means that the data is also outside of the report. This is the easiest and the most affordable option.

Whos Sees the Results of the Appraisal?

When a written report not necessary, it will mean that the value can be shared after the analysis is conducted. It is important to make sure that you can decide what part of the report structure makes the most sense to you.

When it comes to the results of the process, you can ensure that you maintain confidentiality, so that you results cannot be released unless you give express consent.

How to Become a Commercial Real Estate Appraiser

The job of a real estate appraiser has already been outlined clearly above. Many of appraisers work for banks and others work for mortgage companies. There is good income to be made in being an appraiser and there is a lot of research out there to show that many make over $100,000 per year.

1. Find out the state requirements to become an appraiser in your area. There are requirements that are different in every area. It is important to make sure that you have experienced in your area and learn what you can do. With a certification or with a license, you need to take all the classes and make sure that you have done the work for the required number of hours. Here are the national requirements.
    a. Licensed Commercial Appraiser: 2000 hours, 150 license hours.
    b. Certified Residential: 2500 hours, 200 education hours.
    c. Certified General: 3000 hours, 300 education hours.
2. You must have a college degree: Most states will require your proper certification. You are going to want to take courses in finance, economics, business, and more.

You will need to talk to your student adviser. You will need to know what program you need to do in order to be successful.

3. Go to All Training Courses: There are required training courses that you must take. You will need to make sure that you are able to pay your tuition, as well as take the classes when you need to.

4. Spend Time Working as a Trainee: You need to take the time to learn the craft, and that means that you need to work under a certified appraiser to get some hours in. The hours that you are going to need are going to vary by state.

5. Take the Certification for Your State: This is a great way to ensure that you can have all you need to do an excellent job for your clients. You will also have to sign off on an important code of ethics.

Chapter 8: Organizing and Arranging Deals

Before you can organize and arrange deals as a commercial real estate agent, you must become one. Here is what you need to know. You can make a lot of money as a commercial real estate investor. However, it is in no way to make quick money. The skill sets that are involved in this career path include endurance, as well as ensuring you are ready for a long marathon.

What Do I Need to Know About Income?

The income is based on commission. There are some firms that have a salary and other will let you also bring in future commission's earnings. But like residential agents, you may have a 3% fee on all sales. The agency is going to take about 35-40% of the total fee.

Deals can be hard and take a lot of time. It could be around six months to a whole year for everyone to decide on a price and that means that the paperwork can take a very long time. Leasing takes way less time, but it can take awhile for you to get your full commission.

If you are all right with getting paychecks from time to time and knowing that you may not close some deals, and others may take about six months to close. You are going to need about six months to a year expenses so that your expenses are covered during the time you have no cash flow. That fund is super essentially at the beginning of your career and when things slow down.

If you want to be successful, you will need to be a great salesperson. The best agents know everyone who is in the industry. This means that you need to be comfortable introducing yourself anytime. You also need to be comfortable with other aspects like being persistent. It is also important to make sure that you are ready to hop on opportunities when they show up. Ensure that you never leave a client behind.

Agents must be completely comfortable with the process of getting strangers to do business with them. In addition to that, most clients are super busy and that means it may be a high maintenance business relationship. In addition to all of this, it is very important to make sure that agents retain all their rights and that they are willing to make all their future transactions with you.

Maintaining and making all the business connections are critical to the process. That means that it is going to be a lot of long nights and days.

There will be a constant process of rescheduling meetings.

What About Education to Become an Agent?

Every state has its own requirements. It is important to make sure that you can pass a written test. It will be given after all of the course work. Most states will ensure that you have passed between 30-90 hours of total courses. The degrees may also mean that you are able to pass this part of the requirements. There is a lot of course work that can be done online. The license itself must be renewed every two years.

Reading all of the best publications out there is another way to ensure that you are always in the loop on the newest changes, as well as the information you are going to need to do a great job.

What About Work Environment?

Most agents work in the urban areas. Some also work out of their homes. The job is fast paced, and it can be very stressful. It is important to ensure that there is a way to limit as many distractions as possible.

How to Negotiate Your Deals When You're Buying and Selling Commercial Real Estate

When it comes to buying commercial real estate that most important thing you need to know is that is it is one of the most difficult types of business you will ever do. It is a transaction that is expensive and could be full of all kinds of unforeseen expenses. It is important to know everything that you can about the property so you are able to make a smart deal. Here is what you need to know:

1. You need to be able to negotiate with the seller. That means that you need to make sure that you are able to go through the process of making an evaluation with them and know what you need and how you can handle it.

2. Know Your Needs: You need to ensure that you can negotiate with the seller in a way that is very clear. You will also want to ensure that you are able to go through all of the steps that are necessary to have the evaluation for the building.

    a. You need to ensure that you are aware of the location and that means you need to know the setup and the value of it. In addition to that, you need to think about all the accessibility of the building and more.

b. The space you are going to need is also very key and it is important to look at growth as well as decide how much space you are going to need before you get organized. That means that you are going to need to organize yourself effectively before you can move.

c. You need to know your budget and set it appropriately. That is because you need to know what it is that you can afford. You need to know what you can do in order to have all the best financing options. You will need to know how long it is going to take the bank to review your transaction and you will be able to ensure that it is handled.

3. Find Good Advisers: You need to make sure that you are making a good investment and that means that you're going to need to have people who know the market and who knows what you are going to need. Working with a great lawyer will also ensure that you have a good process as well as a copy and paste relationship with

someone who you can do a lot of good work with.

4. You Want to Have a Wide Net to Save on Process

In the market of today, it is important to make sure that you can get an affordable price and a lot of that taint comes with the talent of negotiation. You are going to need to do the following.

    a. Go to more remote sites so that you can get more affordable real estate.

    b. You are going to also be able to afford all kinds of bargains as well to have certain buildings designed. You want to make sure that you are staying away from buildings that have odd designs and that are going to make them harder to sell.

    c. Work to ensure that the property is being sold. When there is a repossessed or a distressed property the value may be lower, and you may be able to get a better deal.

    d. You want to make sure that you are looking at a building that may have more square footage than you need. It may more than you need but you may be able to make a special deal to afford more for your dollar.

5. Look at the Site with Care

When you are looking at properties you need to do so when you are going to make an offer in advance. That means that the more that you know about the property the better you are going to be able to make a good deal.

a. Make sure you know about all the allowable uses.

b. Make sure you are aware if a space needs to grow as well as what you can do in terms of restrictions as well with the space.

c. Bring a few jay people to look at the space with you and look at the renovations that may be needed to accommodate the space.

d. Ensure that you also have your own contractor with you who is going to go through the site with you and allow you to make all the key components that you need like the roof and other issues clear.

e. Find out about the age of the building as well as knows what to expect in terms of whether the area is getting better or worse.

f. You also want to know if the building has any people itself who are in it and if the leases that are in the building are going to expire.

    g. Make sure that you are also working to know all the other vendors about the value of the building.

6. Make a good offer. After you have completed all your homework, you need to make sure that you are considering all the following things.

    a. You may be able to get a better deal at the end of the period if you make an offer that has fewer conditions. That is because there are a few things that you may not need to consider.

    b. You may also want to ask for vendor finance as it is supposed to be available for you to look at all the transactions out here.

    c. You may also see that some owners are interested in a deal that will allow you to sell the building or rent for a part of the space. There are many different combinations you may have.

7. Before You Sign: Make sure that you are going to go through the entire due diligence exercise which will mean that you are able to ask for the tax statements as well as all

the repairs that have happened on the building in the past five years.

In addition to this, you will also want to get any information that there may be for a kind of environmental assessments. There are for the issues of contamination, as well as other issues that you may have. You may need to have everything looked at again by an agent so that you can have the assessment done for any by you.

In addition to this, you will also want to get any information that there may be a kind of environmental assessments. There are for the issues of contamination and other issues that you may have. You may need to have everything looked at again by an agent so that you can have the assessment done for and by you.

Chapter 9: Dealing with Banks

Anytime that someone must borrow money there are good parts and there are bad parts. This is very true when there is an issue with the credit worthiness of all the individuals who are a part of the transaction. The reason for this is that there can simply be a bad bet on someone who has bad financial problems in the past.

The Art of Negotiation and Getting Great Deals

When you are dealing with a bank and with making a sale or closing a deal, it is critical that you know what you can do to ensure that you are going to always close the deal. Here are a few suggestions.

1. Know Your Local Indicators in the Market: You need to make sure that you know and that you understand everything that there is to about the market and the purchasing and leasing in it. That means that you need to know all the local trends and you need to know what you are working with when you are buying and selling. You will be able to have a real conversation with the bank that will allow you to really set things into

motion and to get beyond any struggles you are having as well moving forward.

2. Have Property Knowledge: You need to ensure from the moment you walk in the door that you are always positioning yourself for success. What that means is that you need to look at the following ideas to ensure that you can really stay ahead of the curve.

3. Use Other Case Studies: Here you can ensure that you have all the information that you need to know what is happening locally.

4. You Can Provide Evidence of the Market: By doing this you are going to show all the information around you about the property and other deals.

5. Have Charts and Graphs: You want to have a visual aid that is going to help you to share all your information and do so in a way that is going to help you to support your discussion.

6. Know All of Your Market Pressures: That is going to ensure that you are going to be able to know when there is going to be a change in the market and in the way that things swing.

7. Have Great Negotiation Skills: This is going to mean that you can hone your

responses and make sure that you are on top of everything that you need to know before you are in the office doing business.

8. Know the Transactions From All Sides: You want to know that you are going to be able to have the best outcomes on both sides of the transactions so that you are going to be on top of all of the questions and answers that are a part of the process.

9. Have Simple Close Steps: Remember that every transaction is going to be a little different but there are many things that you are going to have in common. You want to make sure that you can look at all these details and then work towards the best outcomes.

PART 2: What You Need to Know After Acquisition

Chapter 10: Managing Your Properties as a Business

The key to real success in property management is to be a professional. You need to know what to do in what situation and how you can really make things very successful as well as very lucrative. Here are the most important things you can do as a property manager to make sure that all people are happy.

1. Understand That Maintenance is Super Important: This means that you are going to need to make sure that you are on top of maintaining your property in a wat that will really keep your tenants happy. There is nothing that will turn someone away like a building that is in bad condition. The reason for that is that when things are falling apart, it can mean you are going to have significant problems. You need to look at the outside of the building as well as look at all the repairs that are there that can include the roof, grass, plants, and other kinds of signage. When you are looking at the property other things you need to look at include other issues with the furnishings and the plumbing. If you have very high

standards this part of the process becomes very easy to maintain.

2. Make Sure You Know Everything About Your Leases: You need to make sure that you know everything about the leases. That means that when you have property issues that arise that you know what to do as well as what to expect quickly and easily. You are going to need to have many different agreements with the tenants and that means that you are going to need to know what to expect with each person in the building. You need to know that you are going to have strong leases that will help you as well as your tenants. You are then going to be able to use these as the basis for any relationship with them. You need to look at it and see that the lease includes everything that will make the relationship you have with your tenants as ways as possible.

3. Know All of Your Services and Products Inside and Out: You need to know your lease very well. In addition to that you need to know what it is that you are going to offer to a tenant. You may several different versions of agreements that are going to allow you to make sure that you have all the information that is out there for the provisions and the needs of the people

living there. You need to have different agreements for each kind of client. What you're going to need from a tech company is completely different than what you are going to need for a kitchen space for example.

4. Be Great at Communication: You need to ensure that you are being very clear to your clients and that you are communicating as effectively as possible. You need to ensure that you are getting rid of all misunderstandings as well. That means that you need to let people know when something like a renovation is going to happen. You need to ensure that you are going to share everything with them that you can as much as possible in person. When you cannot do that you can shoot them a quick email which will detail everything that they need to know about the process.

5. Upgrade Your Property on a Regular Basis: Make sure that you are working to keep your tenants happy and that means that you are going to keep upgrading the existing property. By doing so, you will be assured that you can raise the rent and the quality of the building all a bit at a time. You want to also make sure that you are keeping up with

all the technological advances that are out there for your buildings as well so that you are never going to lag your competition. You need to make sure that you are going to function better and that means that your tenants will stay there as well year after year.

6. Have an Asset Management Plan for Your Company: In order to be very successful, the other thing that you must have is an asset plan for your company. An asset plan will assure that you are on top of all your assets and that you have a projection for where you intend for them to be in the future. This is a way to keep you profitable and ensure you have a plan for review every quarter.

Chapter 11: Adding Value to Your Real Estate Business

When you own a business the one thing that you want to do is always find a new way to make it more profitable. There are many things that you can do, which will help you to enhance the value of the property. You need to know what else you can do for a property in order to enhance the property.

1. Add Improvements That Increase the Value: Depending on what the property is, there are many things that you can do which will allow you to increase the value of your property with no issue. You can do things like rehabilitation to the properties as well as make sure that you can add in new things like wallpaper and others. You can also add in things like bathroom fixtures that will help you with the process of improving your units and your space.

2. You May Be Able to Add Square Footage: If you are able to add more room to the space that you are using, you will also be able to rent more of it. Look at the property and see ways that you may be able to add

additional footage and ensure that you have more areas up for rent.

3. You Can Increase the Rent: One of the best ways to ensure that you are able to have a good deal as well is to increase the rent. By doing this you are going to be able to improve the amount that you care getting month to month for the property. You will be able to see as well if there are reasonable markups that you can also be adding to your total investment.

4. Decrease Total Expenses: One of the best ways to ensure that you are going to be able to stay on top of improvements with your property is by decreasing the total number of expenses that you have and looking at ways that you can save money on the property. You could easily look at things like decreasing the use of gas and becoming completely electric.

5. Change the Usage: You may also be able to add or make changes to the existing property to accommodate other additions to the location. Such as allowing some renovations to add additional units or shops in the bottom of a building that may be multi-tenant.

6. Add Amenities to the Property: The main reason that most people rent from a specific

property is because they are looking for amenities and those are what are going to drive most people to a specific property. It is important to ensure you are ahead of the curve and that you have a plan for doing this with your property. What can you add that is going to add value and bring in new tenants?

Chapter 12: To Rent or To Lease?

When you want to rent or lease property to tenants there are a few things that you need to consider. Here are the benefits to leasing property.

1. You will have more liquidity. You are not going to have to worry about making a down payment that is going to be a huge chunk of your income. That will mean that you are going to be able to afford more. You are going to have to pay for an attorney as well as a broker and hire an inspection team.

2. You Will Think About Your Business: When you are looking at a business you are going to have less to distract you and that means that you are going to be able to think about your company alone without having to fret over many other things.

3. Leasing is Easy to Make a Budget For: Since you know what the price is going to be per month, it makes it very easy for you to focus on running your business and having to focus less on the bills. You are not going to have to worry about a lot of unforeseen costs which are going to pop up on a regular basis and mean that you are making constant repairs.

4. Tax Deductions: Rent is tax deductible and that means that you are going to be able to deduct all parts of your business and your expenses over the course of the year instead of only getting that mortgage deduction.

5. You Have More Flexibility: You will be able to have more benefits and breathability when you are applying for a lease and not for a loan. That will mean that you are not going to have to worry about selling a property and if you need to, you can move to a better location.

The Drawbacks of Leasing

1. You Are Not Going to Have any Equity or Appreciation in the Value of Your Property: You are not going to be getting any kind of equity when you are getting a lease and that means that you are not going to be seeing an increase in your wallet there.

2. You Will Not Have Passive Income: You are not going to be the landlord and that means you are not going to be collecting rent from other people. In addition to that you are going to be losing secondary income that you could gain from other resources.

3. Rent is Very Expensive: Rent is a payment that will normally be way higher than you would pay if the property was in your name. You will want to make area that you are looking as well at all off the other costs such as the utilities and more. The cost is very high over time and that means that you may need to reconsider your thoughts here when looking at the numbers.

4. You Have No Control: You are only able to use the space in the time that the lease states and that means that you have no control over the space. You will not be able to decide when it expires or anything else. You must keep paying the rent and have no other way to make any other choice.

When Should I Buy and When Should I Lease?

It makes more sense usually for people to have enough money for about six months of payments before they are going to hit a cash issue. Purchasing may only be a good idea if:

1. You want to rent out the space.
2. You want to remain there for at least 7 years.
3. You want to build equity with the property.'
4. You want to reorganize and use the space.

Leasing is Best If You:

1. Need flexibility to move at the end of a lease.
2. Need to not have a down payment
3. Need to have better deductions.
4. Want to not have to worry about maintaining the property.
5. Want to operate from a space that is too much to buy.

Chapter 13: Doing the Right Thing for You

One thing that is important to note is that one business is not like another and one agent is not like another. You may see a mentor or another person you know run their business in a completely different way. You need to consider what you can do to ensure that you are on top of your own method and your approval process.

One thing that is very different these days is that real estate is changing. What this means is that the commitments that people were thinking that they were going to have for years are becoming quicker and they are becoming leases that are more like the service industry. There are many new models that are different for people who have been in the business for many years. Building occupants are now more like subscribers instead of long term occupants. What this means is that if you want to keep the people there, you must constantly manage the needs of the people who are occupying your space.

People are wanting things like on demand storage and other solutions that are going to allow them to stay ahead of the curve. It is important to look at all the options that are going to help you stay competitive. It will keep you ahead of the curve. Now tenants want to have hotel like amenities and be happy with the experience more than they want to have something that they own.

Reviewing Your Business Model

The thing that will lead to the biggest success in the long term is to create a business plan and not be afraid to review it regularly. You want to ensure that you know what is working and what is not working. When something is not working, you need to put a plan in place to make an instant change. What can you do to make sure that your numbers add up and that you are able to always be on the top of all the needs of the company?

Part 3: Growing Your Business

Chapter 14: Creating a Factory

When you are creating your own company, you are working at building a model that works with everything that you need on a long term basis. Here are the steps you will need to ensure that you have a model that actually will work.

1. Practice the Golden Rule: As simple as it sounds, your key to success is to treat everyone the way that they want to be treated.

2. Remember Your Customers and Clients Are Internal and External: What that means is that everyone that you meet whether they are a part of your business or a person bringing you a delivery, you must treat them as a client. You want to always give the best customer service to everyone.

3. Be of Service: This means exactly what it sounds like. Being of service is about being happy and ensuring that you are always there to do whatever is necessary to help your customers and your employees.

4. Practice the Most Ethical Accounting Standards: Always have detailed records of every transaction and spend time going over all the financial implications and

agreements with everyone who is a part of your financial model.

5. Constantly Review What Works: Make sure that you are looking at what works for your customers and what brings them back for more. Similarly look at what is not working and change it.

6. Have a Customer Database: You are going to need to have a CRM system which is also known as a Customer Relationship Management system. Many of these also have a CMS or a Content Management System that is also a part of the process. You need to make sure that you know what you are doing as well as that you are maintaining all the records of the customers and the records of the systems. This will save you a lot of time trying to look through paper notes. A few things to consider CMS systems will also integrate with your CRM and allow you to push out marketing content to your database. Make sure that you are working with a CRM that has payment protection for your clients, high encryption, and proper security settings.

7. Develop a Marketing Plan: The only way to be efficient is to keep nurturing the clients you have and always looking out for new clients. The way that you do this is by

always bringing in new customers and by keeping the relationships with the old ones. Marketing is the door to all those virtual connections.

Chapter 15: Doing Business with Passion and Purpose

Doing business with a passion and a purpose should be simple. You want to help people and you want to make money. A part of being successful in the real estate world is developing an air of trust as well as of authority. The way to do that is by working on ensuring that you have everyone on the same page with the process of sharing information as well knowing the standards. Here are a few suggestions.

1. Always Be Learning: In the information age, there is no reason to ever be sitting back and resting on your laurels. You need to be constantly learning. A good rule of thumb is to invest in yourself for an hour a day. That can be in the form of podcast or eBooks. You want to make sure you are adding to your education so that you can be a legendary player.

2. Ensure You Have a Mantra: Develop a catch phrase that people will associate with your business and then use it in your marketing. You want people to think about your catchphrase in their sleep. It should be simple and ring true. When you look at all

the great marketing companies across all genres in history, they have a few things in common. One of the biggest is simple and easy to remember phrases. Let that mantra guide your actions, your decisions, and your method of business.

3. Share Your Knowledge: When you are first getting started you are the recipient of knowledge and experience from others. When you reach a certain level in your career, it becomes your responsibility to share that information with others.

4. Be Ready to Always Get Better: Constant education is about constant improvement. Always be ready and open to change. After all, the only thing that is constant is change.

5. Give Back: If a community has brought you a lot of business, make sure that you give back. That means that you need to look at what you can do to ensure that you are always volunteering and making momentary investments. You want to show the community you are a good steward of the business that they have brought you.

Chapter 16: Buying and Holding

When it comes to buying and holding real estate, it is one of those strategies that works overtime. The method is that money and value will increase over time and that makes it a good return. On some kinds of buy and hold it can be as high as 9% a year.

How Does the Plan of Buy and Hold Work?

It works because the idea is rather simple, and it means that the investors buy properties just so that they can get them and hold on to them for a long time. The thing that is important to keep in mind about this kind of investment is that you must find people to assist you with property management.

When you have a buy and hold property it is a way to get involved in real estate that is relatively simple and that will allow you to see appreciation build up over time.

What Are the Kinds of Buy and Hold Real Estate Investments?

When it comes to the buy and hold, you need to think about it in terms of the long-term plan of attack. That means that you need to look at all the kinds of property as well. Here is a quick list.

1. Turnkey Real Estate: This is a piece of property that already has tenants and that will ensure that you do not have to do any kind of extra investment and work.

2. Rental Properties for Vacations: These are a way that you can invest in properties that will allow you to decrease some of the costs of your home.

3. Multi-Family Properties: These are units that have about 2-4 units in them that can be rented out.

4. Apartments: These of course are filled with different units and opportunities to allow you to bring in new forms of revenue because they become equipped with all kinds of options for your vending and parking.

5. Commercial Real Estate: This is a property that you can use for your purposes and ensure that you are going to be able to build with stores and the link.

What Are the Main Benefits of Buy and Hold Investing?

The main benefits of buy and hold are below:

1. Monthly Income Assistance: When you have a buy and hold asset, one of the main benefits of it is seeing that you have many other revenue opportunities for your needs. This is a great source of passive income.

2. Depreciation and Deduction: You will see that there are many tax advantages out there that will allow you to be able to buy and hold real estate. That ensures that you can look at how you can invest and take advantage of that investment.

3. End Up with More Equity in the Properties You Hold: When you have bought and hold investments you are going to have a tenant who is paying your mortgage. What that means is that you are going to have an extra value in your property as well as in your value each month.

4. The Appreciation of the Real Estate: In buy and hold models there is a continued valuation add in the value of the property. It can fluctuate and mean that you are going to have more money in your pocket the longer that you hold onto that property.

5. You Can Get Leverage with Real Estate: When you have bought and hold real estate

you are going to see an increase in the ability to have many properties. What this also will ensure is that you can take out home equity lines of credit as well on your property. You need to ensure that you are going to generate as much passive income as you can.

Chapter 17: Finding the Balance in Your Business

Making a living in commercial real estate is very demanding. It means that you need to look at the number of hours that you have in the day and you need to have a plan. You are going to need to see how much of an investment in your time they both are and then you need to make an educated decision about how you are going to approach each one. When you are working with a commercial client, they are going to be interested in the financial analysis that is a part of the process and that means that you are going to need to share demographics with them and research. You are going to need to work through the process as well as the research and show them what they want to know about a property as well as about the local people.

What Does the Average Day Look Like for a Commercial Agent?

The average day is very different from other kinds of real estate. You need to look at all the following.

1. Making cold calls to clients.

2. Looking at lease payments and other locations in your area.
3. You will spend time looking at the math as well for your area and for the breakeven numbers.
4. You will also spend time looking at the market trends.
5. You will spend time looking at all the hot properties that are out there with your name on them.

Commercial real estate will give you a lot of amazing checks, but there are less than there are in residential real estate. You will need to look at the deals and understand that the sales cycle is much longer, and the process of due diligence also takes way longer.

You Cannot Be Anything But a Star

When you are in the commercial market you are going to get a lot of attention. You need to make sure that you are going to have a great database. You to deliver business with your contacts if you move from residential to commercial.

Chapter 18: Continue Learning and Growing

One thing that is critical to your success as an agent or an investor is to continue your education. Look at the degrees and see what you can do in order to receive more education. That is going to mean that you need to continue your learning and education. Here are 10 pointers that will help you.

1. Dedicate an hour a day to learning and growing. Like any skill you need to have about 10,000 hours practicing before you are a master. The best way to do that is the daily grind, but it is also continuing to learn more about what interests you.

2. Take Continuing Education Classes: Many universities offer the opportunity to continue your learning in your trade and to make sure that you are up on all the trends and changes. What they also offer these days is that most of the courses are remote.

3. Stay on Top of the Bleeding Edge of Technology: You need to ensure that you are on the bleeding edge of tech so that you are going to have all the best options for your business. When you have a way to learn about new ideas you want to always

bring them into focus. Read about other software programs for marketing as well as other options out there for your CRM system. Staying on the bleeding edge will help you to come up with the easiest and the best system to share with your clients and save you money. One thing that every businessperson needs to be aware of is the propensity to buy a software and let it sit on a shelf and never be used. That is simply lost money.

4. Listen to the Feedback Your Clients Give You: Take the time to work with your clients and get their feedback. When you do that, you are going to learn what works best for you and what you can do better. Develop a feedback system that allows you to make constant improvements to your business as well.

5. Learn About New Approaches and Theories: One thing that is helpful as well is to always be learning about all the new theory and approaches to the business.

6. Make a Daily Commitment: One of the most important things to do is to make a daily commitment to your clients, excellence and to only improve a bit at a time when working with your clients.

7. Look at NAR Courses: One thing you must do as well is to check out all the options out there at NAR. The National Association of Relators has many free and paid options for courses you are going to want to take.

8. Understand Education Means Higher Commissions: When you continue to learn you are going to be in a place that you are going to learn how to bring in more clients and more sales on a quicker basis.

9. Learn How to Be Gracious: Learning your people skills in a profession like real estate is just as important as learning your academic ones. You need to make sure that you can spend the time that you need to be a professional and to ensure that you are always becoming more of one.

10. Education is an Investment in Your Future: Although in the moments you are taking a class you don't want to or other similar circumstances, it may not feel like it. You are going to invest in your own future when you continue to learn. Realize there will be costs. When you see a thing that is going to bring you a solution to a difficult problem you want to do all you can to learn as much as possible.

Chapter 19: Diving In

The most important thing that you can do is just drive in. When you do that you need to always refer to yourself as a commercial real estate agent. Here is what you need to really be successful.

1. Have a Marketing Plan: You need to have a content marketing plan that will allow you to define what kind of content you are creating and where you are sharing it. You need to review your plan weekly.

2. Create a Business Plan: Look at your plan and define goals of where you want to be and review that goal book on a quarterly and daily basis.

3. Make a Code of Conduct for Your Business: Ensure you and everyone you work with and do business with are following your code.

4. Create a New Resume: That new resume should focus just on your commercial real estate business and your skills.

5. Create a New Simple Website: This will draw people back to you and ensure that you have a site that will help you grow your clientele.

6. Update Your LinkedIn Profile to show your status.

Remember that diving in means that you are making a 100% commitment to your new role as a commercial real estate agent. You need to think of it as a critical part of your identity.

Finding and Choosing Vital Team Members

One of the most important things you will do to make your business successful is to add the right team members. As you continue to grow, you will want to think about the positions you will need. You may need for example:

1. An office manager: This can be a full-time local resource, or it can be a virtual resource who works with you occasionally. Either way you need to make sure that you are working with some one who works well with you and is very detail oriented. This person will help you schedule appointments, reach out to clients and assist in the admin tasks of your business.

2. A Social Media Specialist: You are going to need someone to help you with marketing and that means finding someone who knows all the platforms. When you hire this person, they can be local, or they can be virtual as well. You want to ensure you also have a great working relationship with them

and that they are on board with your marketing calendar and plans so that you can grow the business.

3. Other Agents: As you continue to grow, you are going to want to work with other agents if the workload is too much for you to deal with on your own. You need to sit down and think about the kinds of people that you want to hire. One of the best things you might want to think about is hiring someone who is new so that you can assist and pay back the help you got along the way. You may also be able to bring in a trainee appraiser and allow them to work with you while they are fulfilling all the other aspects of their learning.

You want to personally test your new people and ensure that you are going to have a team that is willing to buckle down and help when it is necessary. A team that cannot work together will cause more issues than it is worth. That is regardless of the talent and the productivity of the team altogether.

Underwriting Considerations by Property Type

When it comes to the issues of underwriting, there are many things that must be considered when you are rating a property. A few of them include the following list that will ensure that you are going to not have any issues.

1. The Repair Issues: It is important to ensure that if there are any issues with the property or the maintenance that they are being dealt with as quickly as possible because it is important to ensure that the building is in great condition over the course of the building. This is important to the underwriter so that they are going to know the kind of behavior that should be expected in the future.

2. Important Notifications: When there is something that is wrong with the property it must be handled right away. When it is it will mean that you are going to be able to have your potential for loss evaluated and dealt with. You will want to have an analyst at the location as soon as possible to act on the issue. This is going to show the underwriter what the procedure is when there is an issue and how fast it can be dealt with.

3. General Risk Issues: There will be data that has to be looked at by the underwriter that will be related to the area. This will be important data that explains things like flammable liquids on the property or other

issues cut as wildlife, damaging floods, an earthquake zone or more. The information allows there to be an accurate evaluation of the issues with the area and to ensure that there are no mistakes in underwriting the property.

4. Estimates of Loss: When there has been an issue with a loss on a property there needs to be a way to look at what the potential losses could be such as in the situation of a fire. You need to know what to expect and ensure that you are going to have the insurance that is required with the fire.

5. Replacement Costs: There are many studied s out there that are very underinsured, and it is important to know what the actual replacement costs would be if there were an issue. So, the more educated you are, the better that you are going to be able to approach a method for ensuring you have enough insurance. In addition to this, there are many companies that do not want to have an underwriting without the correct insurance, so it is a lot to consider.

6. Improving Ways of Reducing Risk: It is important as ell to look at all the ways that you might be able to reduce risk and find other ways that you might be able to save other kinds of hazardous conditions from

becoming a problem. You are going to want to look at all the fire protection as well as suggest ways that improvements can be justified.

7. The Construction of the Building: A bug part of underwriting is looking at the property itself and determining how you might want to look ay how the building would endure if it was exposed to fire. It is important that it understands all the building classes so that all of it can be looked at and handled. Here are the classes:
   a. Frame
   b. Attached Masonry
   c. Not Able to Combust
   d. Masonry that is Not Combustible
   e. Modified for Fire Resistance
   f. Fire Resistive

8. Occupancy of the Building: It is important to know about all the people who are living in the building as well as the business that is happening there. When looking at this, it is possible to also see the information in the following ways.
   a. The number of issues with combustibility in the building.
   b. The ranking of the contents in the building that could lead to

issues and damage to merchandise.
   c. The square feet of every floor and level.
   d. The locations of all the fire extinguishers
9. Fire Protection in the Event of an Emergency: It is important to look at the public and the private outlines and sectors for protection. When it comes to the public protection, there is an ability to look at all the issues such as the fire department he waters supply and many others to see how programs can be done to reduce the risk. When looking at private protection it is important to look at the placement of all the assets like sprinklers in the building and ensure what else can be done to reduce the total loss.
10. Special Hazards: One thing that underwriters also must keep in mind is all the possibilities out there for special issues. When you are looking at a commercial property that means ensuring that you are looking at the flammable possibilities as well as all the other things that are in the location and could cause you an issue.

Resources to Check

When it comes to finding the best resources, you want to stay on NAR. Which is of course the National Association of Realtors. They have an entire section of their website that is dedicated to keeping its agents up to date on the important published information out there and the most current trends. Click Here: https://www.nar.realtor/research-and-statistics/research-reports/commercial-research to see the most important research.

A Few of the Resources Available to You Include:

1. 2019 Commercial Lending Report: This is a list of all the financing conditions out there this year. It also looks at all the sources, the respondent's information and the conditions of the deals.
2. Commercial Member Profile: This is a report that talks about the business as well as all the information of the individuals that are a part of NAR commercial organization. In addition to that, it shares important information for NAR.

3. The Commercial Real Estate ALERT: This is a report that tells you all the primary risks and issues of the commercial industry.
4. Commercial Real Estate International Business trends: he information here talks about the state of the markets and outlines the information that is from the previous year.
5. Commercial Real Estate Market Survey: This is a market that takes you through all the markets and ensures you can see all the issues and trends.
6. Commercial Real Estate Market Trends and Outlook: This is a quarterly report that really has its hand on the current moment since it comes out quarterly. It looks at all the issues that are upcoming and the trends of the day.
7. Commercial Real Estate Outlook: This is a quarterly publication that looks at all the trends as well as the fundamentals of the investments in the market.
8. Expectations and Market Realities in Real Estate: This is a report that looks at all the markets, the capital as well as the sectors that are growing the most at that moment.
9. The Life Kind Exchange Survey: This is a yearly report that looks at one of a kind exchanges and informs the audience about

investment that are similar and happening in each market.

Source: https://www.nar.realtor/research-and-statistics/research-reports/commercial-research

Conclusion

Starting your own business is something that most people spend their entire lives dreaming of. One thing that you must realize though is if you want it to be successful you must take total ownership of the process as well as total responsibility for the success or failure of the business. By learning and taking total responsibility whether you have your own LLC, or you are an agent or appraiser, you are vested in your success. Understanding that the market is hard and not an easy way to get rich over night is also going to be the attitude that you maintain as well while breaking into the business. One issue that many have is that they are looking for easy ways to ensure that they are going to be able to make money in a flash. This is the way of the marathon and not the short sprint. Being successful is all about the golden rule and that way that you want to treat people.

Continuous improvement will help you to ensure you are on top of all your need to be successful. You now have all the tools that you need to take advantage of the education and the opportunities out there for you. Get ready to take the next step towards your family's stability as well as yours. Creating an empire that is left behind by your family and making it in commercial real estate is the American dream. It is also a way to ensure that there will be stability for everyone else and the way to really make it for your family.

When you have done all your need to do to build your business and get it going, the key is to continue in constant pursuit of excellence and always raise the bar. How can you be serving your customers better? How can you serve your community better? What software solutions are you not using that will help you to automate your marketing and your outreach?

One thing that is also very challenging is that there are only so many hours in a day. Of course, everyone has things that they want to do like spend time with family and friends. You should think of the business as a short-term hard investment that is going to net long term results for you. If you are ready to see all that can be offered by real estate, it is important to ensure that you are ahead of the game in your proactive approach to growth. Another key thing you must remember is that if you do not set goals and constantly review them you are not going to be able to stay on top of your needs or the needs of your business. A dream without an expiration date is just a dream. That means that you need to be willing to push yourself and have reviews of your marketing plan and your business plan. Always look towards growth and innovation to be the next thing to take your business forward. Working with others to ensure that you also have a network that is going to perform for you is critical to your success. You never know who it is that is going to introduce you to your next client. Get ready to shine when you are working all the time to grown and to expand.

Living and working by a code of ethics is going to win you fans and new clientele. Word of mouth and successful testimonials from people you have helped will pay their weight in gold. Spend time doing all you can to foster a culture of help and service to everyone that you meet, and you are going to be successful. The other thing that will drive your success or your failure is informing people about what you do and how you do it. You need to ensure you have a great marketing approach and that you are thinking of yourself as a resident expert on commercial real estate. Just because you are an expert however does not mean that there should not be a constant process of striving to become the best you can be in every field.

Remember that by helping others and perpetuating greatness you will see your business grow and boom. Make the commitment that is required to be completely successful if you want to know that you are going to go far and that you will be able to define the trajectory of your business and your life. When executed properly you will never be in a situation again trying to determine where you are going to get the investment from to accomplish a major task. The commission as well as the payoff happens when you fully commit to your work at hand. Taking the time to show people that you care as well as always helping others is the secret sauce in commercial real estate that leads to long term commissions as well as financial stability. Be ready to be of service.

Glossary

1. Adjoining: Next to another property.
2. Agent: A person who assists with the processing or sale of real estate.
3. Assignee: The person a contract is made out to.
4. Assignment: The process by which a contract is assigned from one person to another.
5. Build Out: The construction additions and improvement to a space.
6. Building Permit: This is a permit that allows a government to build...
7. Cancellation Clause: This ensures that a lease allows for one party to cancel the other party's responsibility.
8. Capital Improvement: This is an investment in the property that will improve the overall quality of the property.
9. Capitalization Rate: This is also known as the CAP Rate and is the total value when it is divided by the current sales price. This is used to have an idea on how fast an investment will pay for itself.
10. Certificate of Occupancy: This is issued by the government and states that a building is ready to be inhabited.
11. Chattel: These are household property of the occupants of a location.

12.CAM: This is the amount that is charged to the renter and the base rent of a location.

13.Commissions split: This is the breakdown of the money hat is earned between and agent and a broker.

14.Contagious: This means that here is touching in one property and another along a border.

15.Contingency: This is a requirement in a contract that must happen before a contract is final.

16.Covenants: These are the restrictions and the limits to which use of a property may be enforced.

17.Deed: This is a written instruction that is the title to a property.

18.Deed Restriction: This is an imposed restriction that limits the use of a property by someone there.

19.Default: This is the failure to fulfill an act on the property/

20.Transfer: This is the delivery of one place to another or from one entity to another.

21.Ejectment: This is the action that is required to get back property from someone. That is what happens when there is no relationship that is left between the renter and the owner.

22.Eminent Domain: This is the process that is used to condemn and to get property for public use. The government must recompense the owner for appropriate use.

23. Endorsement: This is the way that one person signs the back of a check.

24. Escrow: That is the agreement between all parties that shows certain funds are released at a certain time. That will ensure that there is an object that must be handled as well with the completion of that occurrence.

25. Estoppel Certificate: This is an agreement that is handled by taking out the mortgage. It is the owner releasing the property to the new owner.

26. Eviction: This is the removal of a tenant by force or by law.

27. Eviction Proceeding: This is the process by which the landlord must remove the tenant.

28. Exclusive Agency: This is an agreement in which one broker has an exclusive right to represent the owner or the tenant. This is used between the original and the broker who is on the leasing commissions.

29. Fiduciary: This is a person who represents someone on financial matters.

30. Fixtures: This is a property that is a part of the land.

31. Grace Period: This is the time that is necessary when there is an action that occurs like a default.

32. Gross Lease: This is a use of a property wherein all the charges are paid by the landlord which is included in the ownership.

33. Hard Money Loan: This is a loan in which the borrower will receive the funds that are a part of the real estate that has been secured with a commercial loan.

34. Holdover Tenant: This is a tenant who is in possession of property after the lease expiration.

35. Incompetent: This is a person who is not able to handle his own affairs by reason of medical issues.

36. Instrument: This is a document that shares the rights of all parties.

37. Irrevocable: This is a document that cannot be changed or altered in any way.

38. Joint Tenancy: This is an ownership of a property by two people and that means that each person has the right of survivorship.

39. Judgement: This is an act that is issued by a court that is related to the rights of a person.

40. Landlord: The person who rents the property to the tenant.

41. Lease: The agreement and contract that spells out all the terms that are a part of living there.

42. Leasehold: This is the interest a tenant has as stated in the document.
43. Lessee: This is the person who has signed the lease with the landlord.
44. Lessor: This is a person who rents a property to a tenant with a lease.
45. LOI: A letter of intent is an agreement between parties to move forward with an agreement.
46. Listing: This is when a contract is between a tenant and a principal that contracts the agent to provide services for the property.
47. Loss Factor: This is the percentage of the space that is lost because of walls etc.
48. Mandatory: This is something that must be handled as specified in a written document without any kind of leeway.
49. Market Price: This is the price for a property.
50. Meeting of the Minds: This is a meeting and a discussion of terms that ensure that all parties are on the same page with what they expect from a contract.
51. Net Lease: This is also known as a triple net lease. This is when the lessee pays not only a fixed rental charge but everything else on a property as well such as the maintenance.

52. NDA: This is given to prevent himself from being evicted if the property owner does not pay the mortgage.
53. Notary Public: This is an officer that can witness documents.
54. Obligee: This is the person who will get the benefit of an obligation.
55. Obligor: This is the person who is performing an obligation to another person.
56. Open Listing: This is a property that is given to a broker without the liability and compensation except that there will be a buyer who is ready to buy that property.
57. Option: This is a right that is given to a property that allows certain terms for a specific time.
58. Percentage lease: This is a lease that is based on a percentage of the sales that are made on the location.
59. Personal Property: This is anything that belongs to a person and that is not real estate.
60. Power of Attorney: This is a written agreement that allows a person to act as an agent on his behalf.
61. Principal: This is the employer of an agent.
62. Quiet Enjoyment: This is the right od a tenant to use property without the disturbances of the landlord.

63. Real Estate Board: This is an organization who has member s that are all brokers.
64. Real Estate Syndicate: This is when partners form an LLC to be a part of a real estate venture.
65. Real Property: This is land and all kinds of improvements that are on the property outlined.
66. Realtor: This is a phrase which is used only by someone who is a part of the NAR.
67. Rent: This is the compensation from the tenant to the landlord for the property use.
68. Restriction: This is a restriction of use that is specified in the lease.
69. Revocation: This is the process of taking back an authorization that was given before.
70. Rule of Thumb: This is a benchmark that is used in the real estate world.
71. Situs: This is the physical address of the property.
72. Tenancy at Will: This is a license to occupy a location at will.
73. Tort: This is a wrongful act by a party.

www.ingramcontent.com/pod-product-compliance
Lightning Source LLC
Chambersburg PA
CBHW071650210326
41597CB00017B/2167